This book has been produced to accompany the **Animals** unit
of five programmes in the **Stop, Look, Listen** series
broadcast by Channel 4 Schools.

The programmes were produced by Moving Still Productions for
Channel 4 Schools and first broadcast in Spring 1997.
Stories adapted for television by Tim Fernée

Published by Channel Four Learning Limited
Castle House
75-76 Wells Street
London W1P 3RE

Illustrations by Alan O'Dwyer, Eileen Carpio and Suzanne Arnold
Art Direction by Mike Bell (Dublin) and John Burke (London)
Stories re-told by Bridget Rendell
Designed by John Burke
Printed by The Bath Press

ISBN 1862151652

ANIMALS

ANIMAL STORIES FROM AROUND THE WORLD

THE WREN: THE KING OF THE BIRDS 2
A story from Ireland

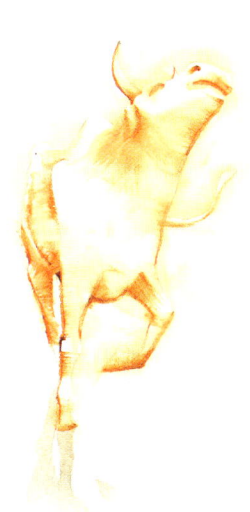

BISWAS THE BULL 10
A story from India

ANANCY THE SPIDER 18
A Caribbean story

THE CAT 26
An international story set in ancient Egypt

THE LAIDLY WORM 34
An old English story

We birds had a great gathering.

From the woods and the forests,
the seas and the lakes,
the mountains and the hills,
we all gathered together to choose our king.

'Now remember,' said the owl,
'I'm the referee and whoever can fly the highest in the sky
shall become the king of the birds.
Is everybody ready? Then let us begin. Ready, steady...'

'Ahem!' interrupted the golden eagle.
He was the biggest, fiercest
and most powerful of all the birds.

'I have a question. When I have won and I am king,
will I get a crown?'

Well, that annoyed everybody, although everybody
secretly believed that he would fly the highest and become king.

Everyone that is, except me, the wren,
the most beautiful of all the birds.
I had a plan!

'Now are you all ready?' asked the owl.
'Are you steady?' cried the owl.
'Go!' screeched the owl.

Everything grew smaller and smaller
as we flew and flew, up and up.
The higher we flew, the further we could see.

One after the other the birds grew tired and gave up.

First the small hedge birds and the birds of the trees
gave up and flew back down to earth.
Then the swallows and larks, the strong flying geese
and ducks gave up and flew back down to earth.

At last, even the soaring hawks and the seagulls,
who fly through the strongest storm, gave up
and flew back down to earth.

From the ground, it must have looked as though
only the golden eagle was left in the sky,
flying higher and higher. As he rose above the clouds,
even the eagle's great wings began to tire.

'I've won. I've won!' he cried.
'No bird can fly higher in the sky than I.
I am the king of the birds!'

And with that, he closed his wings to dive back down to earth.

At that moment, when he was too tired to go on,
I flew out from my hiding place
among the feathers on his back.

When he saw what I had done
he tried furiously to fly back up.
But he was worn out
and I wasn't tired at all.

I flew up and up.
Higher than I had ever flown before.
Higher than any wren had ever flown before.
Higher than any bird had ever flown before,
or has ever flown since.
And I sang and sang,
up there alone in the clouds.

And that is how I, the wren, became king of the birds.
Not for being the biggest of the birds, which I am not.
Nor for being the fiercest of the birds, which I am not.
Nor for being the most beautiful of the birds, which I am.
But for being the cleverest and for tricking the eagle,
who everyone wanted to see tricked.

BISWAS THE BULL

I was born early one stormy morning
into the heat and the dust of an Indian farm.

When I was a calf I didn't know my own name.
In fact I didn't even know what sort of animal I was.

As I grew, I learned my name was Biswas, which means the trusted one,
and I would trot towards the farmer when he called.

10

One day, as the sun rose and the cock crowed,
I set off from the farm to see the world.

I climbed the long, low hill at the edge of the farm.
I passed the tall coconut trees. Then I came to a big pond
that looked to me as vast as the sea.

11

Suddenly, I heard a thudding
and crashing over the land;
and a squelching through the mud;
and a splashing in the water...
...of hooves
...like mine.

Here came a herd of animals
with horns... like mine.
And tails... like mine.

And four legs... just like mine.

'I must be one of them,' I thought.

Into the water I jumped after them.

But instead of squelching and splashing and floating...
...I slithered and stumbled and sank.

And that's how I found out
I was certainly not a water buffalo!

I left the water buffalo in their muddy
pool and set off for the forest.
I loved the smell of the flowers and
the shade of the trees of the forest.

Suddenly, I heard a tremendously loud noise.
A stupendously large creature was squirting me
with water from his enormously long trunk.

I didn't know what sort of animal he was,
but I knew I was certainly not one of them.

Terrified, I ran from the forest
and didn't stop until the sun
was high in the sky.

I grew hotter and hotter,
and hungrier and hungrier,
and more and more lonely.

Suddenly, I heard the sound of my name.
'Biswas! Biswas!'
The farmer was calling me and I trotted towards the sound.

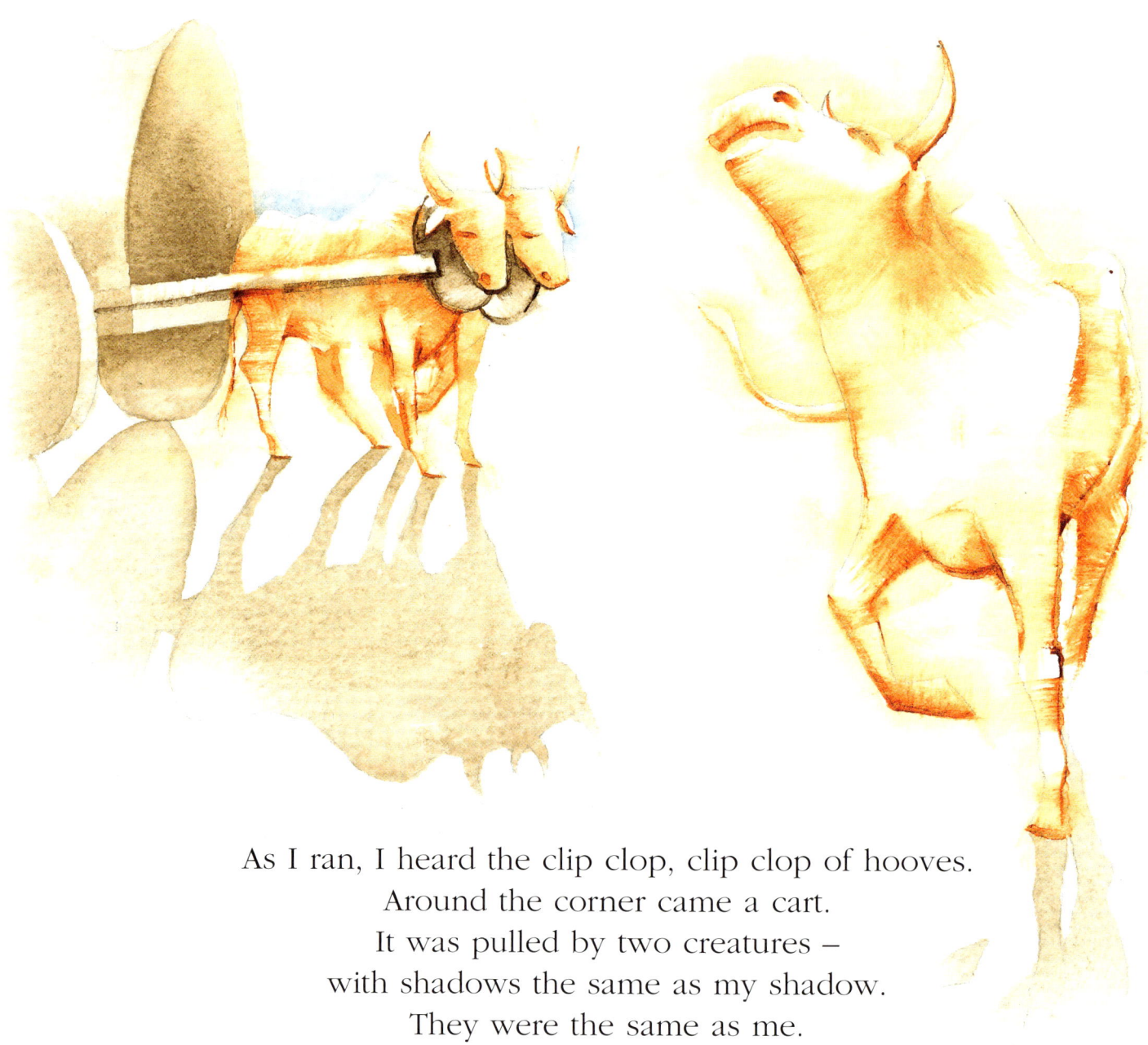

As I ran, I heard the clip clop, clip clop of hooves.
Around the corner came a cart.
It was pulled by two creatures –
with shadows the same as my shadow.
They were the same as me.

It was then that I knew I was a hump backed bull
and that I was no longer alone.
I let out the loudest, happiest bellow of my life.

The farmer came running towards us from around the corner.

And the grown-up hump backed bulls
bellowed as they had never bellowed before...
to welcome me to the great family
of Indian hump backed bulls.

ANANCY THE SPIDER

My great grandfather, Anancy the spider, hated the cold and the wet.
He loved the sun and the bright colours of the Caribbean.

He loved all the good things in life. But although he was clever,
he was lazy. And he didn't want to work for any of those good things.
He would look around and see all the other spiders repairing their webs.
But he left his own web for his son, Tikuma, to repair.

He thought work was boring and beneath him.

'Get wise,' the others said to him.
This was all too much for Anancy and he turned to God.
'Oh Jah, make me wise,' he prayed.
'Make me very wise, wiser than anyone else.
In fact, give me all the wisdom in the world.'

'What a greedy prayer,'
thought Jah, but he smiled
and said, 'I hear your prayer, Anancy,
but I cannot simply
give you wisdom.
You have to go out into
the world and sort out for yourself
the wisdom from all the lies
and foolishness that you hear.'

'No problem, Jah,' boasted Anancy.
'Picking sense out of nonsense
is my speciality.'

And so my great grandfather became the first news reporter in the Caribbean. He interviewed everyone...

...the goodies and the baddies,

...the cops and the robbers,

...and, of course, the spiders and the flies.

And when he had gathered together all of the wisdom in the world,
do you think he shared it? No, he kept it all to himself
to make him wiser and richer than anyone else in the world.

But the more pleased Anancy was with the wisdom,
the more afraid he was that someone would steal it.
He didn't trust anyone, not even his own family.
So, he decided to hide it where no one
would know where to find it.

The next morning he got up earlier than ever before
and took the big iron cooking pot from the kitchen.
He threw all of the wisdom into the pot
and set off towards the forest with it on his back.

But Anancy did not know that his wife was up at this time to feed
the baby spiders, and that Tikuma was up and about and already working.
When his wife saw Anancy, she turned to Tikuma.

'Go after your father and see what he is doing
with my cooking pot,' she said.

So, followed by Tikuma, Anancy staggered through the forest
with the cooking pot.
He went to the tallest tree, where he planned
to hide the cooking pot full of wisdom.

Stopping at the foot of the tree,
he wondered how he was going to climb to the top
with a big iron pot on his back.

'Just put it down and I'll pass it up to you,' shouted Tikuma.

Anancy was so startled by the sound that he dropped the pot!
All the wisdom spilled out and spread all over the world.
And that is why today everyone
can have some of the wisdom if they want it.
You just have to sort the sense from the nonsense.

As for Anancy,
he felt so ashamed
that he ran off
and hid on the ceiling...
which is where he can be found
to this day.

THE CAT

Long, long ago, when all the animals were wild,
who do you think was the wildest animal of all?

Yes of course, it was me, the cat.

We knew nothing about people,
but sometimes at night
we would gaze at the light
where they lived, and wonder.

One by one, wild dog,
wild horse and wild cow
set off into the night
towards the light.
They never came back.

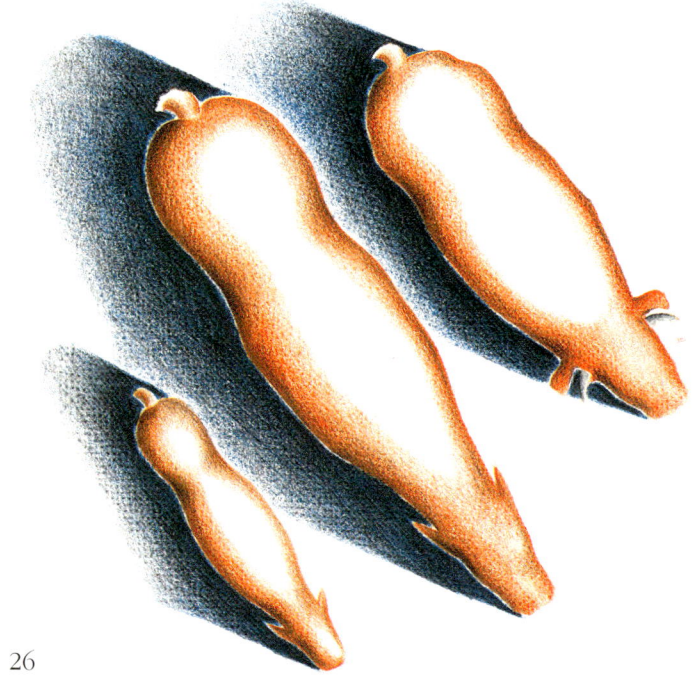

Everyone began to grow afraid. Everyone, that is, except me.

Silently and stealthily, I crept through the countryside, towards the light. There I found a little mud hut. A woman was sitting quietly outside, while a man snored noisily beside her.

'May I enter your lovely house?' I purred.
'Are you tame,' she asked, 'like dog and horse and cow?'
'Not I,' I replied, 'I will always be wild.'
'Go away then,' she said, smiling.
'Off you go back into the countryside.'

I tried again. 'How can someone so wise and beautiful
not let me into her lovely home to sit by her warm fire
and drink her delicious milk?'

Eventually we made a deal.

If I could trick her into saying
something nice about me,
she would let me into her house.
If she said nice things about me twice,
I would be allowed to sit by the fire.
If it happened a third time,
I would get milk three times a day.

'Did you hear that?'
I said to the house. And off I went
into the countryside as wild as ever.

When I returned to the house, the man was away hunting.
The woman was milking the cow and the baby was crying.
I tickled the baby under the chin with my tail.
The crying stopped and the baby laughed.

'What a good cat you are,'
the woman said.
Suddenly, the door of the house
swung open and let me in.

The woman stopped smiling and sat down at her spinning wheel. The baby started to cry again. I took a ball of wool and bounced it and chased it; I jumped and I turned until the baby laughed again.

'What a clever cat you are,'
the woman said.
The smoke from the fire
blew into the room, lifted me up
and put me down in front of
the blazing fire. Hmmm... lovely.

The woman was angry now.
She vowed she would never praise me again.

It grew dark, but not so dark
that I couldn't see out of the corner of my eye...
a little mouse.

I sprang from my place by the fire,
grabbed the mouse and ate him.

32

'What a swift cat you are,' said the woman.
Just as she spoke, the milk pot tipped over onto the floor.

'Oh, you win,' sighed the woman.

And that is how I got my place by the fire.
And when I feel like it, I go out at night to the wild places
and walk by myself. As wild as ever I was.

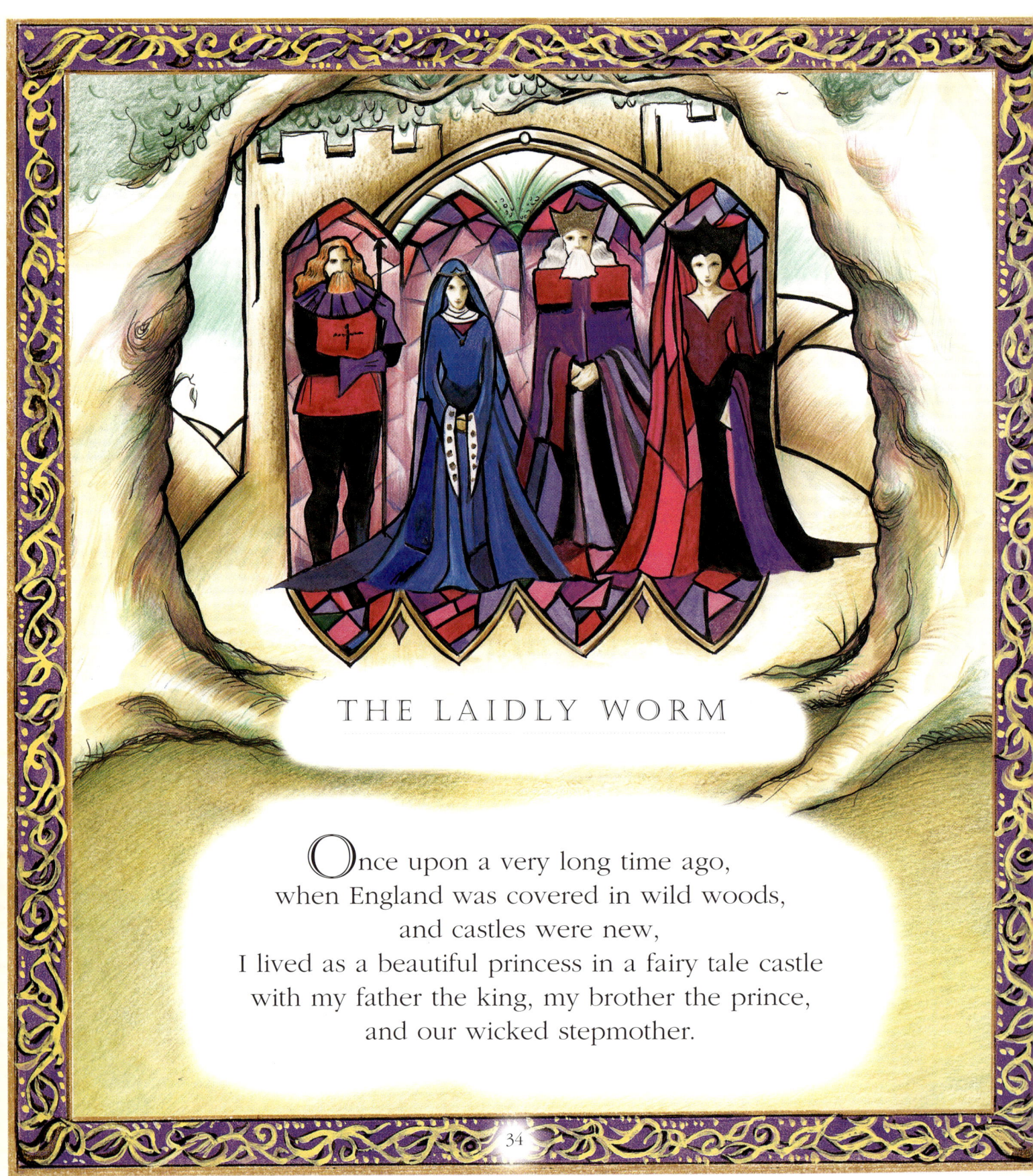

THE LAIDLY WORM

Once upon a very long time ago,
when England was covered in wild woods,
and castles were new,
I lived as a beautiful princess in a fairy tale castle
with my father the king, my brother the prince,
and our wicked stepmother.

Now, our stepmother was jealous of my beauty.
So on the day my brother set off to seek his fortune,
she crept down to the deepest darkest dungeon, where she
worked her magic and changed me into a terrible dragon!

At least, people called me a terrible dragon.
I preferred to be called the Laidly Worm of Spindlestone Huegh.

Although I still had the heart of a beautiful princess,
I had the body and the hunger of a terrible worm.
As I hunted and prowled at night
the people came to fear me.

They went to a good witch
to ask for help.
He told them,
'Feed the worm with milk
and it will no longer
hunt at night.
But be careful,
for only the worm knows
where the princess is
and only the prince
can free her.'

So the people fed me, the Laidly Worm,
with milk and sent for my brother
the prince.

He built a long ship from the wood of the rowan tree,
which is stronger than any witch's magic.
He filled it with soldiers and sailed it home.

From the high tower of the castle,
my wicked stepmother saw
the prince's boat approaching.
She used her witchcraft
to raise a terrible storm
but she could not sink the boat.

Still under her spell,
I was forced to guard the harbour
and chase off my own brother.
But the prince was too clever for her.
He returned secretly, coming ashore
and seeking me out.

He led his soldiers towards me,
not realising who I was.
I wished with all my heart that he could see me
and know that I was his sister. My wish was granted.
He saw me and knew who I was.
He laid down his sword and kissed me,
and with that I was changed back into a princess.

As for my stepmother,
she knew nothing could save her now.
My brother touched her with a wand of rowan wood.
She began to shriek as she shrivelled up
and changed from a wicked stepmother
into a Laidly Toad.